# Making the most of your Maryland auto insurance policy.

Jobeth R. Bowers, Esq.

ISBN: **0692335218**
ISBN-13: **978-0692335215**

# DEDICATION

This book is first dedicated to those clients who I had previously worked with and who were victims of automobile accidents that were not their fault. These people for one reason or another were not only the victim to the negligent act that caused their injury or injuries, but also did not have adequate insurance in one way or another to afford them the recovery they truly deserved. The weight of these numerous situations on my mind was a major motivation to writing the original edition of this book with Attorney Marc G. Snyder back in 2011, and continues to be the purpose in my updating the book now in 2015. This book is for you, and for anyone else who wants to be certain to protect themselves against future possible injuries caused in an automobile accident.

# CONTENTS

# ACKNOWLEDGMENTS

I would not be where I am today without a number of people who have helped me learn about this profession, and furthermore to develop a care and concern for the clients that I have worked with in the past, as well as the clients I will continue to work with and advocate for in the future years of my career. To name anyone specifically would be to set myself up to leave names from the list. You know who you are, and you know the impact you've had on my career, and what you've done to shape my desire to help out anyone that I am fortunate enough to reach with this book, or by coming across them in my day to day practice of law.

Thank you all.

# 1 ABOUT THIS BOOK

I entered the legal profession nearly a decade prior to writing this book. These years have been spent in a variety of roles, beginning as a simple file clerk, growing my knowledge of personal injury law to the point where I managed a high volume Baltimore City law practice, before beginning law school and eventually becoming a lawyer. In some capacity, I have been involved in close to five thousand personal injury claims throughout this timeframe. I have worked on some of the largest auto accident cases, with incredibly severe injuries, as well as some incredibly minor accidents that many law firms would consider rejecting because the value of the claim and the estimated fee would not be worth their time. One role that I played in almost all of my positions within the business has been some degree of work directly with the client. In some cases, it was very entry level-gathering information about injuries, medical treatment, and insurance company claim or policy information. As office manager I was often charged with the difficult, but rewarding task known as "putting out fires" or answering to and handling client complaints when they would arise. I note this job to be rewarding, because I have always taken a great deal of value in the relationship that clients have with their lawyers and the other staff at the law firm that they've hired. The opportunity to solve a problem is the opportunity to build another solid block in the foundation of what could be a long term attorney client relationship. Most attorneys would love to have a practice that is built on word of mouth referrals, but they neglect to put in the time with their current clients to earn the luxury of that good word spoken, and the resulting referrals. Since the first opportunity I had to work directly with clients, I recognized the value of doing right by that client, and in that moment treating them as if they were the only client the firm had.

As I learned more of the "ins and outs" of personal injury cases my involvement and concern with clients quickly shifted to their auto insurance choices. The more I learned, the more I realized that the clients as drivers of vehicles with insurance had the ability to purchase certain types of insurance that would have significant impact on their personal injury recoveries, and most importantly the money that a client would put into their pocket at the end of a personal injury claim.

I encouraged the attorneys that I worked for over the years to educate their clients on getting better insurance so their claims would be worth more if they were to get into another accident. Some of these lawyers could care less, as I noted their concern was their fee, not their client. Others would discuss briefly with their clients, but go no further to help improve their clients' situation. In 2011, I worked with a Baltimore based lawyer named Marc Snyder, to write the original 2011 edition of the guide to buying auto insurance in Maryland. Marc understood the importance of educating clients on the important pieces of their auto insurance policies. We both understood that those individuals who took advantage of the insight and suggestions we provided would have a much better financial outcome if they were ever in a future accident. Whether through the information in that 2011 edition, or though direct conversations within Attorney Snyder's office, we were able to help hundreds, if not thousands of clients over the years to be more educated about the various parts of their insurance policies, and to make changes that would help them in the future.

Most of the laws that determine how automobile insurance works, and what coverage is and is not required are dictated by the Maryland General Assembly. The General Assembly is the State's elected legislative body. They meet each year in Annapolis beginning in January, and serve a 90 day term though to the middle of April. Occasionally they are called back for a "special session" to work on legislation at the direction of the governor. Each year in the Maryland legislative session a large number of potential bills involving automobile insurance, accident claims, and other traffic and safety laws are introduced. Not all of these bills become laws, and those that do often are changed or amended several times prior to passage. Due to this, the auto insurance law and rules are often changing. Just around the release time of the 2011 edition of this guide, the legislature changed the rule on the minimum liability insurance that someone had to buy in Maryland. More information on the specifics of liability insurance will be covered in that later chapter. Myself, and a large group of lawyers from an organization called the Maryland Association for Justice were instrumental in meeting with the Delegates and Senators in Annapolis to bring about this much needed update to the state's insurance rules. This was a minimum insurance requirement that had not been updated since 1972!

This guide will serve as a comprehensive overview, much like the 2011 edition did. It will also provide updates that have happened over the past 4 years, as well as a few additional chapters on specific topics that were not covered in the first book, but are often asked by clients and readers of the book. There is no need to purchase the 2011 book if you are reading this book. In fact some sections of this book will be merely a freshened up and edited version of the old book. Keep this guide with you, and stay up to date on any future updates to the book or though our website. The goal is to keep those who are interested in knowing how to protect themselves up to date, and with the best insurance possible should the unfortunate occur.

As always with these books, I thank you for investing in this guide as well as taking the time to educate yourself on how to better protect yourself.


Best,


Jobeth R. Bowers
Maryland Attorney


Disclaimer: The information and suggestions within this book are not to be mistaken as legal advice. Insurance policies are different for every person, and the variables that influence one's insurance eligibility and rates are numerous. This book does not intend to or imply any attorney/client relationship. It is also not an opportunity or invitation to purchase insurance from the author, as the author is not a licensed insurance agent or insurance underwriter. The author is in no way connected to the insurance industry in any way that would qualify him or those in his office to sell or officially quote insurance prices. Information or suggestions within this book are based merely upon hypothetical situations, in order to explain the way in which various aspects of an insurance policy impact a potential personal injury claim in Maryland.

# 2 TYPES OF INSURANCE COVERAGE

In the state of Maryland there are several different parts that make up an automobile insurance policy. Each one covers different types of "losses" that could involve an automobile. Each part is separate, but all contribute to a single automobile policy. It is important to note that some of the coverage that will be described is mandatory in Maryland, while some of the coverage is optional. Each instance will be explained individually. The main types of coverage in a Maryland Auto Insurance Policy include:

1. Personal Injury Protection (PIP)
2. Collision Coverage
3. Liability Coverage *
4. Uninsured Motorist
5. Underinsured Motorist
6. Comprehensive **
7. Rental/Roadside Assistance ***
8. GAP Insurance

*Liability coverage is the only truly Mandatory coverage in Maryland

\*\*Comprehensive coverage does not typically involve an injury, and will not be covered in this text.

\*\*\*Rental coverage and Roadside assistance coverage are handled differently by each company offering them, and will not be covered in depth in this book.

I will discuss the approximate costs affiliated with each of these types of coverage, but exact pricing is different for each person and for each insurance company. Factors that contribute to differences in price include different companies, accident history, ticket history, age, gender, type of vehicle, where you live, and credit score/credit history. In Maryland, unlike some other states, credit scores are a significant factor in insurance rates.

Each insurance company evaluates their pricing differently, and this document will not attempt to determine the specific criteria for acceptance or pricing for any company.

It is important to work with your individual insurance agent in order to compare pricing for different policies and types of coverage. You can also explore insurance pricing on several internet websites designed to provide policy quotes. Keep in mind, these quotes that you find on the internet are often approximations, and actual policy premiums could vary greatly between an online quote and an actual premium.

The author and any contributors to this guide are not insurance sales people, and are not authorized to sell insurance. You will need to contact a licensed insurance professional to discuss any details or premiums with that person.

# 3 PERSONAL INJURY PROTECTION (PIP)

Personal Injury Protection or 'PIP' is a common part of your automobile insurance policy. While it used to be mandatory in the State of Maryland, it is now possible to waive this coverage.

PIP insurance is used when you are in an automobile accident and injured. PIP will pay your medical bills and lost wages, up to a certain amount, determined by the policy you purchase. I suggest that you add as much PIP coverage to your policy as possible, as it will save you much headache should you be in an accident. PIP coverage is usually sold in increments of $2,500, with the Maryland maximum coverage of $10,000.00.

Typically the price difference between $2,500 and $10,000 is only a few dollars a month.

Let's say, for example, you are in a serious automobile accident and injured badly. If you are injured badly enough to be taken to Shock Trauma, your medical bills will be over $5,000.00 before you ever leave the hospital. A few more months of rehab and your bills are likely to be close to, if not more than $10,000.00. If you've got the highest PIP coverage, most of these bills will be paid before your attorney even discusses settling your case with the insurance company of the driver who caused your injuries. Also, if you have passengers in your car that are also hurt, each of them can be covered up to the same amount*.

## What does this mean?

Simply speaking, it means more money in your pocket at settlement. Every dollar that does not need to be paid toward a medical bill from your settlement means another dollar in your pocket. *This is specific to Maryland insurance and accident claims. This advice may not be relevant or even correct in other states. If you live in another state, please contact a professional there to determine the best course of action for your out of state policy.*

## What if I miss time from work?

Easy: PIP insurance typically covers time you miss from work. Our office will provide you with a wage & salary verification form that your employer will complete. That, in addition to any 'off work slips' from your doctor will allow us to collect from your PIP insurance for the time you miss from work. Note: PIP insurance covers 85% of your lost wages.

*Passengers who have chosen to waive PIP on their personal policies will not be eligible to collect PIP from your policy.

## Will my insurance rates go up if I use my PIP?

No, your insurance rates will not go up because you use your PIP coverage. If you are at fault for an accident your rates may raise, but not because of using PIP coverage. The only real reasons that an insurance company is permitted to raise your

Making the most of your Maryland auto insurance policy.

premiums would be if:

1) They raised rates across the board or;
2) You were at fault for an accident or received a traffic violation.

### Can I use PIP if I am at fault for an accident?

Yes. Accidents happen, and if you happen to contribute to the cause of an accident, it does not mean you did not get hurt. If you have injuries or miss time from work, your PIP insurance can cover these the same way as if you were not at fault for the accident.

What should you do?

I suggest that you contact your auto insurance agent to discuss the possibility of increasing your PIP coverage. Get quotes on how much it will cost to add PIP if you do not have it or to increase it if you already do.

### Typical pricing for PIP Insurance:

Typically adding PIP insurance is relatively inexpensive as compared to the coverage it actually provides to the recipient. The minimum coverage allowed in Maryland is $2,500.00 per occurrence, and will cost as little as $7.00 per month depending on the company and criteria used to set prices.

Increasing PIP coverage to $10,000 per occurrence will increase premiums as little as a few dollars per month. It is highly advisable that anyone who has the financial means to increase their PIP coverage to do so. It will ultimately protect you if you ever are in an accident that causes injuries to yourself or to any passengers in your vehicle.

# 4 COLLISION/RENTAL COVERAGE

Collision coverage is typically the most expensive coverage to have as part of your insurance policy. This coverage, while optional, is designed to pay for any damage to your vehicle in any accident in which your vehicle was driven. Most often this applies to when there is an automobile accident. Collision coverage is only used to repair damage to the vehicle covered by the policy. Collision coverage can be used whether you are at fault for the accident, contribute partially to the accident, or not at fault at all for the accident. Typically this coverage is accompanied by a deductible ranging from $50 to $1,000. A deductible is money that you would pay out of pocket before the insurance company would begin making payments toward repairs to the vehicle.

For instance: If there is an accident that causes $3,500.00 worth of damage to the vehicle, you may choose to use your collision coverage to repair the vehicle If you have a $500 deductible, you would pay $500 out of pocket toward the repairs, and your insurance company would cover the remaining $3,000. If your deductible is only $100, you would pay $100 and your insurance company would pay the remaining $3,400.00 Note: The lower your deductible, the more expensive your policy will be.

**The accident was not my fault, why would I use my coverage to fix my car?**

This is a very common question asked of attorneys and insurance agents alike. In an ideal world, the damages will be paid for by the at-fault insurance company, and there would be no deductible paid out of pocket. However, insurance companies often operate very slowly. They also typically require that they speak to their insured driver before they will make any payments. If the driver who caused the accident is avoiding his insurance company, you may have to wait several months for your vehicle to be repaired. If you use your collision coverage, your insurance company should begin arranging for repairs the same day.

**Why should I pay my deductible if the accident wasn't my fault?**

This is a question even more common than the previous. This question becomes somewhat more complicated, but is a continuation of the previous. Let's say, for example, you are in an accident that is not your fault. There is approximately $3,500.00 in damage to your vehicle, and you have a $500 deductible. You allow your insurance coverage to arrange for repairs to the vehicle and pay the $500 deductible to the body shop. Your insurance company, while they are looking out for you, is in the business of making money. In an effort to make their money, they will begin a process called 'subrogation' where they contact the at-fault insurance company and get their money back. When they get their money back ($3,000) they will also get your deductible back ($500). While it may be nice to have the $500 in your pocket right after the accident, if the other insurance company is stalling, it may be considerably nicer to have your car repaired within a few days of the incident.

**The Insurance company cut me a check for $800, and my vehicle is drivable. Can I just keep this money?**

You can, but you shouldn't. In Maryland insurance companies deal with so many accidents on a daily basis that they often have adjusters who make preliminary estimates based on what they can see from the outside of a vehicle. These damage estimates are often much lower than the actual cost to repair, but are accurate based on what the adjuster is taking into account when writing the estimate. When you take the vehicle, and the preliminary estimate check to a body shop, they will often find additional internal damage that was not originally seen by the original estimator. The extent of the internal damage can be quite severe, and some times can have structural damage to your vehicle that isn't immediately noticeable. If you take that $800 check, cash it, and buy a PlayStation of an Xbox, and your vehicle has additional problems (likely due to that internal damage no one has seen) you will be stuck with the damage, and be required to pay for it out of pocket. There may also be additional issues when it comes time for your attorney to negotiate the settlement of any injury claim resulting from the same accident. Lower damage values to vehicles tells insurance companies and those negotiating settlements on their claims that the accident "wasn't that bad" and they automatically feel that the passengers in that vehicle "couldn't be too hurt" and often offer much lower settlement amounts.

**Where can I take my vehicle for repairs? Should I go to the insurance company's shop?**

In Maryland, you are allowed to select the body shop you want to repair your vehicle. Insurance companies have ongoing deals with their "preferred" body shops, but those are often driven by the desire for the insurance company to keep the cost of repairs low. Sometimes, but not always, this can result in corners being cut, and inferior repairs being done on your vehicle. While they will tell you the work is guaranteed for a certain amount of time, you probably will want the work done right by a shop that is looking to repair the vehicle for your best interest, instead of running back to a shop to have the same thing fixed several times.

### How Do I get a Rental Car? Who pays for it?

If you have opted for additional rental coverage on your automobile policy, it will dictate the terms of the coverage. These policies usually limit the rental car in two ways: first, there is usually a daily limit on the amount to be spent on the rental car, and a limit to the number of days the rental will be allowed. These vary by policy, and will be something you will need to ask about or read specifically. If you are having your vehicle repaired by the other, 'at fault' insurance company, they will cover the rental car, but may have similar limits in place as to time and price. Any additional rental needs or upgrades to the vehicle rented will be the responsibility of the renter.

### Typical Pricing for Collision Coverage?

As mentioned previously, collision coverage is the most expensive part of an insurance policy. The most common deductible is $500. The average cost of collision coverage with a $500 deductible is as little as $40 per month, where as decreasing the deductible to $100 could increase the premium to as much as $75 per month! While it is clearly ideal to have the lowest amount of out of pocket expense if there is an accident, the deductibles and associated premiums for collision coverage are clearly up to the individual's desires and affordability. It may be more important to have the coverage in case you need it, than it is to have the lowest deductible, especially if a lower deductible causes the policy to be unaffordable.

# 5 LIABILITY INSURANCE

Liability coverage is among one of the only truly mandatory coverage types in a Maryland automobile insurance policy. It covers what it states: Liability. If you are the cause of an accident, and the result of that accident is injury or damages to another person or their property, it will be covered by your liability coverage. Liability coverage, like the other coverage types, comes in a variety of different coverage levels or values. On your insurance coverage sheet, or declaration page, it may look like one of these:

$30,000.00/$60,000.00/$15,000.00**
$50,000.00/$100,000.00/$25,000.00
$100,000.00/$300,000.00/$50,000.00

As you see, there are 3 different numbers associated in your liability coverage. The first value is the maximum dollar amount that your policy will pay out to an injured driver/passenger of another vehicle. The second value is the maximum dollar amount that your policy will pay out for all injuries resulting of a single accident. The third is the maximum dollar amount that your policy will pay out to repair damages to other vehicles or property caused in the accident.

Making the most of your Maryland auto insurance policy.

If you cause an accident resulting in severe injuries to another person, your liability coverage is what will pay for their damages. It is possible that if you do not have adequate coverage, tan attorney could sue you for excess damages, if the damage is worth significantly more than the limits of your policy. This could result in seizure of your home, boat, vehicles or even have wages garnished. It is important to have adequate coverage, especially if you own property. Remember, insurance is designed to protect you in the instance of an accident.

Recently, a Maryland Insurance Agent representing Farmer's Insurance posted a comment on a blog post at http://www.bowerslawmd.com/blog suggesting that if you are a homeowner, the minimum coverage you should have is $250,000/$500,000/$100,000. This provides a great deal of coverage to protect you and your assets, should an unfortunate accident happen. At this points, most insurance companies will offer to sell you an umbrella coverage policy of $1,000,000.00 for as little as $10/month. Not a bad idea to make sure you're fully covered, especially with a cost so low.

\*\*NOTE\*\* The 2010 Maryland General Assembly passed HB825, which raised the mandatory minimum automobile liability coverage from $20,000/40,000 to $30,000/$60,000 effective on all new policies and renewals after January 1, 2011. The last time in which the mandatory minimum liability coverage was updated in Maryland was 1972.

# 6 UNINSURED/UNDERINSURED

Uninsured (UM) and Underinsured(UIM) Motorist coverage are often times the most important and least understood coverage on a policy. It is often sold in tandem with liability coverage, and you cannot buy more UM/UIM coverage than liability coverage, but you can buy the exact same amount.

**What does it cover?**
UM Coverage is the insurance that you carry to cover you in an instance that a driver at fault for an accident does not have insurance of their own. This also covers a victim in the instance of a hit & run accident, in which, an injury is involved.

Much like liability coverage, on your insurance coverage sheet, or declaration page, it may look like one of these:

$30,000.00/$60,000.00/$15,000.00**
$50,000.00/$100,000.00/$25,000.00
$100,000.00/$300,000.00/$50,000.00

For explanation of the breakdown of coverage value, please review the liability chapter.

The major difference between liability coverage and UM coverage is that when you are at fault for the accident, your liability coverage pays the victim's damages. With UM coverage, YOUR insurance company pays YOUR damages when the at-fault party does not have insurance.

Underinsured coverage, on the other hand, will cover your damages if the defendant has insurance, but not enough to cover you. For example: If you are badly injured in an automobile accident, and the defendant has minimal insurance ($30,000.00), but your medical bills and expenses are deemed worth $50,000.00. In this instance, the at-fault driver's insurance company would be responsible for paying their maximum, $30,000.00. If you carry additional UIM coverage, your company would then pay an additional $20,000.00 to cover the $50,000.00 that the claim is worth. Initiating these types of claims often have complex requirements of an insured putting their insurance company on notice that they are making such a claim. It is advisable that these types of cases are always handled by an experienced lawyer or law office, so as to not make a mistake in the very detail oriented process that may cost tens of thousands of dollars.

These are all situations where the victim, usually a "good driver", would have been protected had they purchased the proper insurance coverage.

Also important to note: If you are a victim of an accident and the at-fault driver does not have insurance, and for whatever reason you also do not have an active insurance policy on your vehicle (which is a violation of Maryland law), you cannot recover. The fact that the other driver is 100% at fault, or that you were catastrophically injured is completely irrelevant. If there is no insurance, there is no one to pay for the damages. This may be the worst situation imaginable, so be certain to avoid it, as you never know when you may be injured as the result of another's negligence.

# 7 GAP INSURANCE

GAP Insurance is a tricky subject that is always asked about by clients when it is too late to do anything about. It used to be that GAP insurance was almost exclusively sold by car dealers, not by auto insurance companies with regular policies. That has changed in recent years, and that change is one of the main reasons this chapter is in the 2015 edition, when it was absent from the 2011 book.

You have undoubtedly heard the saying that the value of your brand new car is significantly lower than what you paid for the car the moment you take it off of the lot. If not, you might need to get out more. This interesting saying is almost absolutely true. While I am not an investment advisor, nor do I claim to be up to date on what the best investment vehicles are, I can tell you that a vehicle(automobile) is not one of the best investment tools out there. Your brand new car or truck immediately depreciates in value the moment you drive from that lot, and continues to depreciate. In fact, most people who are driving financed vehicles owe more money on the vehicle than the car is worth. Yes, almost every financed vehicle on the road today is under water!

GAP insurance comes into play when a vehicle involved in an accident is deemed to be a total loss. A total loss is a term used when the cost to repair a vehicle exceeds the value of the vehicle or is so close to that value that it isn't worth it to repair. Instead, the insurance company will pay the owner of the vehicle the value of that car, instead of paying to repair it. If you are under water, or owe more money than the value of the car, you'll be stuck still owing that outstanding amount of money.

Depending on the car you own, and the value compared to the loan amount, this shortage can be thousands if not tens of thousands of dollars! Who wants to pay that money for a vehicle they don't even own any more? That's why companies sell what is called GAP insurance. That specific policy will "fill the gap" between the value of the car and the amount owed on the loan. You won't walk away with any money in your pocket from the car, but at least you won't be left owing thousands if not more.! GAP insurance is usually inexpensive, and as previously noted, most new and used car dealerships will offer it at the point of sale. You can also check with your auto insurance company, as more and more of these companies are beginning to offer GAP insurance on their auto policies.

# 8 COMMON MISTAKES MADE

The rest of this guide has described important types of insurance coverage to protect you and your family from injury caused by the negligence of other drivers, but it is also important to describe the common mistakes made when buying insurance that cannot be changed if an accident occurs.

Here is a bulleted list of mistakes that are often made to "save money":

• Waiving PIP coverage.

• Buying the minimum limits of liability coverage because "you're a good driver"

• Thinking that you'll be able to add additional insurance after an accident happens. The coverage you have at the time of an occurrence is all that you will have available to you for that accident.

• Not shopping for new rates regularly. Prices change frequently in the insurance business. It is wise to price shop every 12-18 months for what other prices may be available in your market.

The truth behind waiving PIP insurance is that you only receive a discount on the Personal Injury Protection premium on your policy. Because you can waive PIP for yourself or those in your household(except children under 16) you cannot waive it for your passengers. So even if you waive PIP, if I am a passenger in your car, and we are in an accident, your company will still pay me PIP benefits even though you elected to waive the coverage. Therefore, they end up charging you 50% or more of the premium you would pay to not waive the coverage. Why pay for a benefit you're not getting. Do not waive PIP!

Insurance is only partially to protect you from the mistakes that you or those who use your care make. As noted in the Uninsured/Underinsured motorist chapter, the mistakes that other irresponsible drivers make can play a significant impact on your life if you are not properly protected. If you are a good driver, then having better coverage will not cost you a whole lot. It'll also make sure you're protected no matter what happens because of other drivers.

Any changes made to your insurance policy usually take effect as of midnight the day you make them. This doesn't provide much of a window to sneak in some additional coverage after an accident happens. I have heard stories of drivers who have attempted to do this, thinking they'd get additional benefits. What they actually get is the experience of being involved in an insurance fraud investigation. Most of the insurance tips in this guide are not incredibly expensive. No sense in waiting until an accident happens to change coverage, because it'll be too late.

In the intro section of this guide there is a brief discussion of the legislative process that makes insurance coverage change on a regular basis. For this reason, it's important to be shopping for new rates every year, even if you are only having your own agent check up and make sure you're getting the best rates. Much of the insurance industry that was against the increase in liability limit minimum requirements back in 2010 argued that such an increase would make insurance premiums rise drastically. In fact, the increase in minimum policy limits seemed to make policy premiums go down. It may have had something to do with a lower likelihood of needing to use underinsured motorist coverage, or any other reason that is way above my pay grade.

If you're looking to save money on your insurance premiums, the next chapter provides a few basic tips on how to do this without destroying the protection that you're paying for. Take a look at these, or talk to your agent first before making any policy cutting decisions just to save money.

# 9 INSURANCE BUYING TIPS

15% in 15 minutes or less.
An average of $456 per year.
More than 15% in less than 15 minutes.
Pick your own premium.
$29 cheap auto insurance

These and countless other slogans or pitches have been used recently to drive business to agents and websites for some of the major auto insurance companies. They rarely ever discuss how they're going to save you that money, and what parts of your policy that they plan to gut in order to save you money. Cheap insurance is usually exactly that, cheap! Like most things cheap, it won't be there the way you want it to be there when you ultimately need it.

Here are a few simple tips that can save you a few dollars to a few hundred dollars on your insurance policy without cutting the protection out of it. Speak to your specific insurance agent, as they may have some other specific promotions or discounts that can help in addition to these general tips.

- Pay for your auto premiums once per year.

This may seem daunting, but you can save anywhere from 5%-15% on your policy just by paying annually instead of monthly. You may also get smaller discounts paying twice a year, or quarterly. If you think the money is too much, shop for auto insurance while you're doing your taxes. That way, if you're getting a tax refund you can roll it into paying your annual policy, and still have some money left over!

- Bundle your multiple policies with the same company.

If you have a home or rent a house or apartment, you likely get another discount by having those homeowners or renters policies from the same company. If you rent and don't have renter's insurance, get it. The discount you get will usually pay for the cost of the coverage, and sometimes even be more than the policy, and it'll cut your bill.

- Buy higher insurance limits.

This might seem counterintuitive, but insurance companies determine their premiums based on the potential risk of paying a claim. Many of these companies have computer programs that weigh a variety of factors about you to determine your risk level. Some of these companies' programs will consider you to be "less risky" if you are even interested in higher limits policies. Typically those companies trigger those discounts at the 250,000/500,000 liability limit range. Also, keep in mind that a claim that is worth $20,000.00 will pay out the same on a $30,000 policy as it will on a 250,000 policy, so the bigger policies are often times not more expensive scaled to the amount of increased coverage you get. It's usually a good bargain.

- Be responsible with your driving.

One of those factors above that will increase your risk level will be speeding citations. Be careful, watch your speed, and if you are pulled over it may be worth the money to hire an attorney to help get you a result that isn't a guilty disposition. If a lawyer can negotiate you a probation before judgment on a speeding ticket, it may cost you a few hundred dollars to hire the attorney, but the guilty finding you'd get without the lawyer will raise your rates for at least the next 3 years! It's often cheaper in the long run to hire an attorney to fight on your behalf.

- Clean up your credit.

This may not be true for all insurance companies, but one more big factor that weights on insurance rates is your credit score and credit history. There has been some fight in the legislature to keep this from being the case, but as of right now your credit score can impact your insurance rates.

Following any number of these tips can be helpful in lowering your insurance premiums. Some of them will even increase the coverage that you carry, which means more protection if you are ever seriously injured in an automobile accident. Not all of these tips will be right for everyone, and as mentioned above, your insurance agent may have some other discounts that are specific to one insurance company or another.

# 10 QUESTIONS NOT IN THIS BOOK

This book was designed as a small guide to cover the basics of auto insurance. By no means is it meant to cover every angle of every situation possible. That book would be over a thousand pages, or you could just visit a law library and read the Maryland Insurance Code.

I am honored and happy to answer questions about buying insurance to anyone who calls my office looking for information. It doesn't matter if you are a former client, current client, or have never been a client of mine or my office. I believe that it's important to have a different perspective when making important decisions like buying auto insurance. While there may be others who have different opinions on buying insurance, what you need, and what you don't need, this guide is written from the perspective of a lawyer who works with clients who have been injured in Maryland automobile accidents. The information, suggestion and tips in this guide are very much specific to Maryland law and Maryland automobile accidents and insurance policies. The same suggestions may not be made in other states, nor does this guide contend to provide any information for any state other than Maryland.

Do not hesitate to call my office with a specific question,

or even to schedule a one on one consultation where I can sit down with your current insurance policy, and suggest any changes you may want to consider. I can be reached by phone though my office line: 410-975-7000 or via my office e-mail jobeth@bowerslawmd.com. If for any reason there is not a fast response to either of these, be sure to Google me and make sure I have not expanded my practice, taken on a partner, or otherwise changed the name and number of my practice. While I can update those items on the digital internet, I cannot go back and re-write this edition of this book.

# BOWERS LAW

## A MARYLAND TRIAL PRACTICE

# ABOUT THE AUTHOR

Mr. Jobeth Bowers grew up in Maryland, and has lived here most of his life. Briefly spending time in Rochester New York and Chicago, Illinois for undergrad and post-college work, he returned to Maryland and graduated from the University of Baltimore School of Law. At the time of publishing this book, Bowers runs an expanding law practice focusing on Personal Injury and Criminal defense matters with offices in Elkton, Maryland and Baltimore, Maryland. He is active in his local community, both with pro bono type outreach work, and providing regular seminars that are open to the public on a variety of topics, including buying auto insurance.

**Jobeth R. Bowers**
Attorney

# BOWERS LAW

A MARYLAND TRIAL PRACTICE

224 East Main St
Elkton, MD 21921
P: 410-975-7000
F: 410-834-3560

*Offices in Elkton and Baltimore*

jobeth@bowerslawmd.com
www.bowerslawmd.com

www.ingramcontent.com/pod-product-compliance
Lightning Source LLC
Chambersburg PA
CBHW070357200326
41518CB00012B/2265